Made in the USA
Las Vegas, NV
14 March 2024

87201003R00111